PLAYA STEP YOUR GAME UP

BY

PRETTY TONY

Published by

World Movement Records

www.worldmovement.com

Copyright © 2010 by Pretty Tony

For information contact
lamont@worldmovement.com
prettytonylv@gmail.com

ISBN: 978-0-982876-80-0

www.playasuniversitysygu.com

Printed in the U.S.A

Playa, Step Your Game Up

Rules to the Game of Macking

By

PRETTY TONY

Published by

World Movement Records

www.worldmovement.com

For information contact
lamont@worldmovement.com
prettytonylv@gmail.com

ISBN: 978-0-982876-81-7

www.playasuniversitysygu.com

Printed in the U.S.A

Acknowledgements

Riche Rich, Biscuit, Skip -Tru players, Jay Fisher good lookin fam, Syn City, To Eaze R.I.P true playa, Brandywine, Simone, Stephanie, Heather my muse, chocolate so nice I must say it twice chocolate, Shannon, Barbara, Tina, Teresa, Jasmine, Andrea, yo-yo, Diamond my jewel "la familia", Dahlia my boo boo, Shelly, Blackie, Sonja, Nashia, Nina, Lisa (1st lady), Michelle, Charmaine, Debra, to all the women who took time to love me and care for me, my eternal love, Sarah my dear friend love you. I've spent my life loving women and I've enjoyed the journey. The list of women around the world is too numerous so I send everyone my love.

Preface

As a child growing I was fascinated by women. When my friends were playing games, I would be with grown women listening to their conversations.

My mother told me that on my first day of school while other children were crying and clinging, I saw a cute little girl and took off after her without saying goodbye. Throughout the years, nothing has changed. I still adore and appreciate women.

As the title suggests, this isn't a romance novel; it's a book of truths so much so that there are those that will hate it. But, so what? That doesn't mean a thing. Real talk: this game is being played state to state, country to country, by both sexes—yes, men and women. So everyone needs to claim their own s*#*.

PREACH, LET ME TAKE YOU TO CHUUCH!!

Contents

Truths

Deception, Manipulation, Coercion, Revenge, are not supposed to be associated with relationships but they are *"Real Talk."*

Gladys Knight and the Pips had songs that said, *"Neither one of us wants to be the first to say goodbye."*

Millions are so unhappy. Damn miserable to be truthful and refuse to go their separate ways:

> *"Why are you still with him"*
> (Response) *"I don't know!!"*
> or
> *"Why did you marry him?"*
> (Response) *"He is the only one that asked me."*
> or
> *"She still playing around on you?"*
> (Response) *"Yeah, but I can't leave, we got kids."*

"WHAT!!?" You've been pissed upon and told it's raining! Get your damn mind right.

Time is short and there is way too much living to be done. People like myself embrace our bachelorhood or single life bliss, and say life is a buffet, let's sample. Travel, explore, gorgeous women, good food, fine wine and cigars. Man, check this out: you are what you are, so figure out who you are and get to living your life.

Some women have the *"Elmyra"* syndrome—that

cartoon character on Animaniacs that finds stray animals and smothers them almost to death with her love.

"I'll hug him and kiss him and love him forever and ever." The problem is, you can't change him, he must change himself. "Real Talk." Just the way you can't make a "Ho" a Housewife.

A fool sees and hears what they want to, not what they are being told! Quit talking and listen sometimes and the person next to you will tell you who they are. Out in the streets you must have game. Your personal life ain't no different: you gotta have some game.

"WHY?" YOU SAY.

I'll tell you: because true players have macked, seduced, perfected this gender attraction thing to an art form—better yet, a science. So you best know who you're dealing with and adjust accordingly.

Am I shy guy, today?
Am I intellectual?
Am I thuggish?
Am I suave?
Am I clumsy?

Lets' size her up and make the move. Chameleon capabilities are a must. Life is a chess game of moves and counter moves. The hunt is the thrill—knowing your prey pouncing on it. "PLAY ON PLAYERS." I'm not only a card carrying member, but I am the president and one of the Board members. We are a worldwide club: some are secret members, and some eat, sleep and live it.

Being naïve is the one thing that is a curse for both sexes. If you don't experience, how can you know what to look for?

Predominantly, everyone depends on books, movies, etc. That comes down to parents too busy sheltering and smothering their children. Man, check this out. Start exploring your sexuality and stop being a "CLOSET FREAK." Pastor's daughter or church girls are the freakiest broads out there. Go check the track record.

Players' Creed

Here are some players' codes I'll break down for you.
(Players' alphabet)

A. I'm not mister right; I'm mister right now.

B. You can't out slick a can of grease.

C. Love doesn't see enough, but jealousy sees too much.

D. We don't chase, we replace.

E. Don't sweat me, let me.

F. Don't hear what you want to hear, hear what you're being told.

G. What you see is what you get.

H. I'm like water baby: I got to keep flowing.

I. Do you have mirrors in your pants; I see myself in them.

J. I'm not into relationships; I'm into encounters.

K. Women outnumber men 5-1, so I've got duty to other women.

L. I like my women in bunches, like grapes.

M. I live for today not tomorrow.

N. If she is willing. I'm able.

O. Things are better in pairs.

P. Know your role, play your role.

Q. Set boundaries. If you cross a boundary, you violated "next."

R. Quit talking and listen.

S. Chuurch P. I . M. P
　　　　　 R N Y U
　　　　　 E 　 　 R
　　　　　 P 　 　 S
　　　　　 A 　 　 U
　　　　　 R 　 　 I
　　　　　 E 　 　 T

T. You got to walk my walk and talk my talk.

U. Once I lay the cards out. it's up to you to
　　 play the hand.

V. Appreciate a woman's body, love her curves, caress
　　 her mind, enjoy her time— she's a work of art.

W. Style is mandatory: exude, exclude and entice.

X. When you spit, spit jewels; sow seeds in
　　 her fertile mind.

Y. Know yourself and make sure they know
　　 how you get down.

Z. Get with it or get gone.
　　 N . T . P . P
　　 E A U E
　　 V K S R
　　 E E S S
　　 R 　 Y O
　　 　 　 　 N
　　 　 　 　 A
　　 　 　 　 L
　　 　 　 　 L
　　 　 　 　 Y

Men have been emasculated -- no "Balls" anymore.. Man, check this out, it's a natural order of things: this is a mans world. But somewhere along the line we (men) let women take the lead. Check history -- the biggest wars were fought over two things…

1. Religion
2. Pussy (women)

Solomon lost his mind over the Queen of Sheba, dude. According to biblical text this was the wisest man born. Julius Caesar was obsessed with Cleopatra, Helen of Troy of mythical tales brought down an entire empire, Samson's downfall came from Delilah, Napoleon's downfall was partly due to Marie Antoinette, King David sent one of his finest soldiers to his death to have the dude's wife. How many homies are dead behind pussy or got set-up by a girl?

So you must ask yourself "What do I say?" Always remember: N.T.P.P.

REAL TALK….any way you look at it, you are leasing with the option to buy when it comes to sex and relationships. I can already see some people's faces thinking, "this guy is crude, rude, vulgar etc."

Screw that -- let us examine facts:

A.   Dating entails dining out, flowers, liquor, gifts, movies, jewelry, outfits, helping out on a bill or two. (This scenario goes both ways.)

Cha ching, cha ching.
Cha ching Cha ching,
dollar bills.

B.   Marriage entails paying mortgages, tuition, childcare, car notes, groceries, vacations, credit card payments, medical bills, etc.

C.   Divorce, entails, child support, alimony, court fees, lawyer fees, splitting of assets.

Cha ching, cha ching.
Cha ching Cha ching,
dollar bills.

Even being a player Costs for maintenance: wardrobe, jewelry, ride, manicures, and condoms!!!

Being a true, and I repeat *true* player means a level of independence – yes, it is a must for your ladies to take good care of you. You should have additional sources of income.

That's what separates a true player from a wannabe. A true bona fide, certified, player can lay in bed with one female and be talking to another on the phone, and both women are fully aware.

A wannabe wouldn't answer his calls, let alone have his phone on. A true player always has a hustle, always looking for his next $100/$1000/$10,000 depending on what level of hustle you are on.

You must be self-assured, have self-esteem, keep a swagger about yourself,

The way you present yourself is the way you are treated. Always remember "we don't chase, we replace." So if she isn't willing to play her role, tell her kick rocks.

If your game is tight you will have a replacement already on the line. As a player you don't go for the "oakey doke," meaning:

Rules

A. Nobody absolutely nobody pops up at the crib (house).
B. Nobody answers your phone but you.
C. Nobody touches your property without permission.
D. Don't ask me where I been, where I'm going, who I'm with -- it is not your concern (this rule goes both ways).
E. If you bust my windows, I'm busting every window in your house and burning your car.
F. If you key the paint job on my ride, I'm wrecking your car.
G. If I told what I need, then provide -- or someone else will.
H. I do not tolerate a woman being disrespectful to me, because I'm always a gentleman.
I. **"Always keep boundaries"** and a zero tolerance approach to maintaining them.
J. Gifts you received are now yours; make that clear.

If you are going to live this lifestyle, I do not encourage any kind of serious relationships. This is true because **"hell knoweth no fury like a woman scorned!!**

This will ultimately bring chaos and unpleasantness into your life.

You would be surprised how co-operative women are if they know whassup. Tell them you are a player and allow them the "choice" of dealing or moving on.

Women are very attracted to a man other women want or desire. They want to be the one who tamed the wild beast.

If you are gonna be a player don't half–step!!"

Once you give a woman the choice of "dealing" or "moving on" you've let her know that "this is who I am. Respect my lifestyle and play your role or keep stepping!"

A player doesn't need to play mind games and toy with emotions. Because everyone involved is on the same page and any disruption will bring dismissal, player say what you mean and mean what you say, and always firmly stay in control of your circumstances or environment. If a female isn't with the program, dismiss, delete.

"DO NOT HIT A WOMAN!" If you have to physically abuse her you don't need her. That is ticking time bomb that always ends up with negative consequences, and the only thing negative we need is a "HIV test." REAL TALK PLAYA!!

Most assuredly you don't need a string of Baby Mamas, because child support negatively affects cash flow, "Really though:" If you do have children take care of them -- this is mandatory in the course of your gamesmanship.

Your children are a reflection of you. Women really dig a man that is good to his kids and will gladly chip in on purchases for your child/children.

Now let's go back to the player's alphabet:

A. I'm not mister right, I'm mister right now
This Establishes that you live for the moment and you are not looking for marriage and commitment.

B. You can't out slick a can of grease.
"Look baby you can't run game on me because I'm a player, so save it."

C. Love doesn't see enough but jealousy sees too much.
This is for situations when someone is claiming they love you and didn't know you were a player. This leads to too many questions and constant interference, because then their imaginations start to go into overdrive. Shut that down immediately: "DISMISS, DELETE, AND REPLACE."

D. We don't chase -- we replace.
Keep it movin, pimpin, "NEXT."

E. Don't sweat me. let me.
Make your intent clear by establishing that fact from day one.

F. Don't hear what you want to hear, hear what you are being told.
We all have a tendency to put a spin on what the other is saying:
"I just got out of a relationship and I'm just having fun!";
"We can kick it, but you do you and I'm gonna do me!";

"I'm still trying to find myself!" (You've heard these before huh?)"

Where in any of those statements did you hear the words love or relationship? Hear what you are being told.

Let me school you some more, players. Here it is: let me drop knowledge.

Pussyology 101

Game, Gamesmanship, Macking, call it what you want: it's an art, it's poetry, it's psychology all wrapped up in one Conversation and communication skills are primary.

Ask any woman about having great conversation with a man; you gracefully bypass their defenses.

Practice, practice, and practice. Learn how to hold a conversation and let her tell you about what's on the inside of her. You would be shocked how many husbands don't know their wives are freaks.

Let a woman tell you her insecurities, fears, fantasies, curiosities. Listen, listen, and listen. Appreciate her kindness and learn about reciprocation (player) -- never be selfish.

You have some players who say "you gotta break a bitch." Wrong, WRONG. A woman will hand you the world on a string, if she believes you are appreciative.

Also you have been led to believe that great sex is the key. No, it is only a "PART." Her mind and her heart are the keys. Get in her mind and she will have orgasms by you speaking to her, know how to woo her, know where her spot is (or sometimes her SPOTS).

She will get "wet" by your slightest touch as her body anticipates your arrival. The very thought of you puts a smile on her face, remove all her inhibitions and lets her feel freer with you than any man before or after you. Be her best friend. I've known women that leave their husbands, boyfriends, girlfriends asleep in the other room, just to hear my voice for a moment. They know what I am but they don't care -- around me anything taboo is permissible.

If they need a shoulder to cry on, I'm there. Car broke down, I'll go get them. Short on a phone bill, no problem. 'WHY?" you say.

Simple: because you got to keep the circle complete. "What goes around comes around!!" With women small things mean a lot.

You must possess the ability to read her body language; eyes are the windows to the soul and woman's eyes and body language tell you everything. Even in a nightclub, or out in the streets: watch her facial expressions and her eyes will say "HELLO or "STEP THE HELL OFF!!"

Her body language shows if she is drawn to you or not. It's a massive turn-on when the pheromones and the hormones get to flowing, player. The chemistry just explodes. Be exciting, be naughty, be charming. You are a philanderer, you are a philosopher, and you are even a philanthropist.

Women love a smart man. The philanderer in you makes you taboo. You are a bad boy but you are charming, and good girls like bad guys.

Players' Poetry

Poem I

If I cannot be that which I am
Then what am I to be,
If I cannot be that which I am,
Then what "oh" what am I then
For misery is now my fair-weather   friend,
Will I, shall I, not become I/me,
No one will make me,
or take away from me
That, which I am,
Until I choose to be otherwise,
For I can only be me.

Poem II

"Ode to a woman"
Her scent, her lips,
"Hmm" her hips,
As she sways, her feminine ways,
Just to touch her,
Just to smell her,
Her whisper, her stare,
Just to touch her hair
"Come over here", "Let me whisper in your ear"
Her glow when she sleeps,
Her tear when she weeps,

Head to toe, this girl I must know,
"DAMN!!"
You see player you have to be well rounded, even pimps are poetic

"Look here baby, put your shoe sole on the Ho stroll!!"
"That fool want some honey, he betta have some money."
"The only thing free round here is conversation."
"My money betta be your motivation"
"Yo time betta be his dime"

GET THE POINT!!

Become a wordsmith, become worthwhile, Ooze style, Ooze confidence

"CASANOVA"

No woman respects a man she can push around, Some women are very domineering and if you are a doormat, She will walk on you, take from you, and get "June bug" or "Tyrone."

To handle her sexual needs, generosity is one thing but being a complete fool is another. You have got to carry yourself like a grown–ass man.

I told you earlier don't get pissed on and be told it's raining. Golden showers are not for you player. That's

why women talk about
"Thug loving"
A thug comes through, rough house the pussy and smacks that ass, smoke a blunt and he out.

REAL TALK!!
You don't have to be a thug, just find a balance between Casanova/Thug loving.

Handle your business.

Look, the rest of the alphabet is self-explanatory. This lifestyle isn't for everybody -- real talk. I've seen so-called playas trippin' because they found out one of their girls was with other guys -- get your mind right, **"wannabe"**

"You do not own her"
"You are not special"

If you are a playa you are a connoisseur of delectable, delightful, delicate, sensual beings. We live in the moment and when the moment ends, we gracefully excuse ourselves and on to our next moment, our next encounter.

Check your ego, player. Everything you are doing has been done before, everything you've said has been said before.

"Scire proprie est rem ratione et per causam cognoscere!!"

Translation: *To know properly is to know a thing in its reason and by its cause, we're truly said to know anything, where we know the true cause there of.*

Let that go round and round in your head. Look I'm just passing through dropping some game on you. A teacher never teaches the student everything. There are rules to this lifestyle. Become familiar with them or you will find yourself caught-up, shot-up, and stabbed. They say progress is slow process, but that is only if your game isn't tight.

Poem III

"Hidden treasures"
She said "I'm like a mummy; you have to unwrap me, to get to know me"
So layer by layer I unwrapped,
Age and time had taken some of her beauty,
But man she still had inner beauty,
Not to mention a sexy booty.
What things she revealed,
I felt like a thief as I found her jewels,
For I saw things and touched things
That has long been hidden
"Aladdin!" she would say,
As I made my getaway
And blew a kiss her way.

Poem IV

"Honerella"
As I was standing at the bar,
Spotted her shaking the figure,
Bouncing left to right
To the sound of "Jigga"
Damn got to step to her make her aware of my presence,
Make her aware of my existence spit game at her,
She's playing hard to get have to be persistent,
Gave her a compliment "Aah" got a smile,
Invited me to sit for awhile,
Said she liked my style,
I responded "I dig your whole profile."
Exchanged digits,
Spent a few more minutes,
Gently touched lips,
Placed my hand on her hips,
Squeezed my fingertips,
She said "you're making me hot but I gotta shake the spot."
Seems like the crowd parted as she departed,
In my mind I said "I'll see you soon, mon cherie, so we can finish what we started"

Nightclub Etiquette

To you this may sound like fiction, player, but this is how it goes down.

Corny lines like "come here often?" or "haven't we met before?"

DO NOT WORK!!!

Be tactful in your approach -- never seem thirsty, desperate, just hitting on everything moving in a tight skirt or dress. NO! Be selective it's a numbers game and rejection is a part of the game. Arrive, approach the bar order a gentleman's drink

EG:
Belvedere and Red bull
Capitan and Coke

Or whatever floats your boat as you hold that drink your pinkie finger should be slightly cocked and adorned with a nice pinkie ring. Find a comfortable place to stand, observe the scene, never just gulp your drink sip, savor, observe the sensual beings around you.

See who is observing you, look for eye contact. Women are very coy, player they notice your looks before you notice them, sometimes it's a bump as they go by, asking for a light, a smile across the dance floor. Some are direct: a napkin with a phone number, they ask you to dance You must have a sense of humor to "break the ice" quickly. Be smooth; be sexy, something about darkness, alcohol, music and chemistry between you and her. Make her want you player.

Eye contact is powerful -- don't gawk at her assets, she is waiting for you to drool, **NEVER DO THAT.** Grab her attention and never let it go, but before the conversation closes, let her know you appreciate the way she looks tonight.

Hand her your cell phone, two-way, sidekick, palm pilot, business card, whatever, and let her know that having her phone number is a priority, but let her program or write it down.

Leaving a club with one number is cool, because she might have been a dime piece. But a good night for a player is three or better.

Bonus Chapter

Gamesmanship

Throughout this book I've stressed that this way of life is not for everybody. But if you decide to step into my realm, I'll continue to holla at you. Now as you look at yourself in the mirror, what do you see? Be honest with yourself -- you have got to step it up, man!!

Presentation, preparation, packaging. Learn what colors compliment you, learn what materials feel good and looks good on you, learn about colognes, coordinate your clothing and shoes. Learn what accessories go with a certain look. Do you even know how to knot a tie?

With all this being said, it all depends on what kind of women you are trying to attract. Please, please enough with the fake Rolexes, the oversized cubic zirconias, bro. If you on the bus stop with huge rocks in your ears everyone knows what they are.

Now back to the game,

So you go through all this, but you still can't conversate. Aah, the proverbial Achilles heel of most men. So here are some helpful hints:

A. Hoodrats A hoodie already knows what's up, so your first conversation is about time, place, and condiments (liquor, blunts, whatever) needed for the sex to go down.

B. Older women- depends on their martial status, if they are married, well then you are their escape from the monotony of married life. Make conversation humorous and naughty. Take her back to a time when she was free, freaky, and sexy not doing missionary style every other week. If they are single, then they have been around the block a few times and know what they want. Find out what it is and provide it; they, too, want to feel young again. Play your cards right they might teach you a thing or two. Believe me, women enjoy being the first to show you something. Their generosity knows no boundary.

C. Ms know it all – I do so enjoy miss know it all; she challenges you at every interval. Constant chess game but primarily it is just a defense or reflex taught by previous hurt or her parents. Observe, adapt and adjust: play her game, and when the opportunity strikes rock her world -- because if you don't her looks and tone will become condescending.

D. **Romantics**- Above all else I am enamored with these gentle flowers: the way they kiss, hold you, and touch you, "oooh la la." You must fuel their passion, and fan the flames of their desires. These women often have a fragile heart, "Do not trample over it." She knows who you are and how you get down. They take great care in tending to your needs. Conversations with her should be light, sweet, walks in the park, movies, cuddling etc.

E. **Freaks**- its simple: step-up or shut-up, playa, because she is going to bring it. Don't be talking about what you can do, just handle your business. Talk softly but carry a big stick. She is going to make her sexuality do all the talking, so be careful -- her sexuality will take you on a wild ride. Unless your mind is right, most men think with their dicks. And if your dick is running things she will possess your mind. The vagina is an addictive thing; think about the things you have done to get it. Enjoy, but do not try to control.

F. **Gangsta Boo-** they are a special breed: "bonnie" as I like to call them, down for you come whatever. She talks tough, quick to fight, she will catch a case for you, she will rob, hustle, whatever to take care of her man. When she loves, she loves hard, she demands respect, with her you have to be something she has never had before. She is accustomed to thugs, so use charm, wit, show her things that she never saw before because deep down inside she is still a girl. But though she adores you, understand this: she will always be with a thug. That's fine, because we are "playas" and got to keep it moving.

Look, being a gentleman of leisure requires a certain mindset, I have said this before. We enjoy a good life and with this comes a certain amount of responsibility to the game. Know the rules. When a hunter goes hunting, he knows his prey, where it sleeps, and he makes sure he is equipped. Same thing with women: if you don't know them, spend time with them, talk to them, how can you truly hope to partake of all they have to offer?

Finally for husbands, boyfriends, girlfriends who will undoubtedly read this book, get to know your mate.

Because we gentlemen of leisure are real and we will take your girl from you in more ways than one.
CHARGE IT TO DA GAME!!

Pretty Tony

Now I've given you the basics, see ya in vol. II.
Nah, I'm just joking.

What was presented was designed to spark you, whether you tall, short, fat, skinny, ugly whatever you may be.

YOU GOT PLAYER POTENTIAL!!

PEACE/PROGRESS

PLAY ON!!Email: prettytonylv@hotmail.com